HUMAN FORM

Oliver Dixon was born in Sussex and, except for periods travelling in Europe and Asia, has lived most of his adult life in London. He is a specialist teacher for students with learning disabilities. His poems and reviews have appeared in *PN Review*, *The London Magazine*, *The Wolf*, *Frogmore Papers*, *Long Poem Magazine*, *Blackbox Manifold*, *Gists & Piths* and *New Welsh Review*. He blogs at *Ictus* (oliverdixon1.blogspot.com). *Human Form* is his first book.

Human Form

Oliver Dixon

Penned in the Margins

LONDON

PUBLISHED BY PENNED IN THE MARGINS
Toynbee Studios, 28 Commercial Street, London E1 6AB
www.pennedinthemargins.co.uk

The right of Oliver Dixon to be identified as the author of this work has been asserted by him in accordance with Section 77 of the Copyright, Designs and Patent Act 1988.

First published 2013

Printed in the United Kingdom by MPG Biddles Ltd.

ISBN
978-1-908058-12-6

CONTENTS

Acknowledgements

Thanks are due to the editors of the following publications, in which versions of these poems previously appeared: *The Wolf*, *Gists & Piths*, *Nthposition*, *Blackbox Manifold*, *Eyewear*, *The BowWowShop*.

Thanks to Garth for the cover art, to Tom for robust editing, and to Laurence for unflagging support when I needed it most.

Human Form

To Rob, for many years *the onlie reader*

~

*'That which they are formed from, things return to when they
pass away, as is ordained: for they pay penalty and retribution
to each other for their injustice according to the assessment of
Time.'*

Anaximander, *only surviving fragment*

Skip

Yellow
rusting out-tray
crammed with gutted flats'
interiors — ripped fittings,
once-dear furniture
binned and inert
in the dusty, late winter
sun —

tiny
slip-of-a-thing
dancing past, lifts one
flipflop over the other
with that half-shifting
hop, loops the rope
sky-high and round
in the uncertain
insistent
parabola

of beginning

Human Form

Each morning we wake in a new
configuration: either
you've traded beds in a bumpy noctamble
and my first blink-cum-nuzzle
finds you shrunken, dream-morphed
from woman to boy;

or a nightmare's made him migrate
and upheave me,
and I come-to with feet exposed, arms
buckled in, Pluto and Tigger
my feral bedfellows,
Spiderman-lamp still on in the light.

Or even, he's somehow wriggled between
and spreadeagled,
entangling us in a cubist scrum:
we struggle into consciousness
like a many-limbed Lakshmi assuming
human form; or a ruffled, parodic

Trinity, momentarily conjoined.

Interruptus

Even removal of clothes they undertake
with more than habitual care, not to wake
the small interloper as he edges REM,
vocalising crises far inside his dream
but not surfacing. They inch in, engage
gingerly at first, with the stealth (the image
comes to them) of furtive adulterers
whose lust thrives on flouting what endangers
itself. Fearing the dark weather of his envy,
struggling to contain the avid frenzy
their bodies strain towards, climax gathers,
like a surge far out at sea; together
they swim towards it — but capsize, wash-up half-dead:

the boy stands watching, towering above the bed.

Cityscape with Floating Lover

After Chagall

I wonder you're still there, your prone body
bearing down on mine like a landslide I've no cause
to escape from: you're the sleep itself I can only
submit to piecemeal, like a local anaesthetic,
as you too welter towards sleep and lodge across me
your dense grace, your abstraction. Without duress

muffling as this — so unearthed am I, so attuned
to fine intervals of temperature and noise —

wouldn't that breeze that in the window ums and ahs
surely rifle through me like the intimate
papers jumbled across your desk — or like its glass
of hangdog tulips, dislodge and smash me to bits?

Wouldn't it waft me into the turbulent street
beyond your starfish-ballast and asylum
to where deals are being brokered in smoky
huddles, car-stereo breakbeats cut through — and day
degenerates into sirens, looting, the blue night
dawning across your unmade-up face?

Local History

'Notting Hill had become a looking-glass world, for all the most mundane objects which everyone takes for granted had suddenly assumed the most profound importance. Milk-bottles were turned into missiles, dustbin-lids into primitive shields: two symbols of everyday life turned into instruments of destruction.'

Edward Pilkington, Beyond the Mother Country

I

Early man — hirsute,
  breakfast-averse —
               stomps sockfoot
onto Portobello Rd.
    weathered acoustic
                  aloft —
Hendrixes it
     to atonal smithereens
bawling 'THERE! I
         WARNED YOU!'
just by
    the fish-stall tub
where splintery crab-legs
            writhe out
their dry
     slow
       throes
and a chucked orange

        festered back to green
bursts up
            in smoke
like a pantomime
                    kazam!

        II

Quam bonum in unum habitare
            Royal Borough of Kensington
                and Chelsea motto

    The antique market
at its periphery
    (Acklam Rd,
Golborne) peters out
        into disjunct
                bricolage
splayed on pavements
            for cider-shrapnel

schoolkids rummage
    a biscuit tin
        of action heroes
disfigured
            as amputees fresh
    from Kandahar

a Trellick Tower
    Lee Scratch Perry,
sensi-cheroot
        olfactable from the Grove,
growls jeremiads
against the slow-milling
    grazers, longhaul
pilgrims seeking
        Hugh Grant's
            bookshop-door:

You called me those names

They made me what I am

Jah will bring judgment uponyah

A to Z

Bird, look! you urged, jabbing at the onrush
gusted up with leaves, Rizlas, filaments
of rain. This brown flutterer
looped between, animated as any —
but bird? Only in your
emergent world — mine too, for the snatched
duration of that game: *seize*
what's air-borne, tiny son, before it spirals
back down to earth. The loose,
elusive paper escaped our grasp
almost successfully : what alighted
was this : an index-page
from a worn-out *London A to Z.*

Is it storybook? you said.

Transit

Cloud-forms edging
over, this one
a murmuration of albino
starlings;

this
the ghost of an airship
that came to grief
                    long
before our time

            They seem
all but stationary;
polystyrene mobiles
                    too slow
for our attention span

Are we still the children
who rushed out to the field
    to watch the hot-air balloon
come down,

amazed at how it loomed
to dwarf us,
            half-scared;

then amazed again
to see the huge, cloud-like globe
        topple down,

like a circus-tent
    buckling and crumpling
to the ground:

they folded it up
    into a black Transit
and drove abruptly away.

The Other Side of Silence

'If we had a keen vision and feeling of all ordinary human life, it would be like hearing the grass grow and the squirrel's heart beat, and we should die of that roar which lies on the other side of silence.'

   George Eliot, Middlemarch

   Overcome
by a swarm of sneezes,
as though my nose
           wants to contribute
its own brusque outbursts
      to this sudden commotion
day buzzes with; not sudden in itself,
but I wasn't
paying attention before,
   too many signs bombarding me
with contradictory messages: EAT MIGHTY BRAN!
                     PM DECLARES WAR. WHY NOT
BE A WRITER? Something about
this luminous afternoon
         is adjusting the balance, nudging up
the sub-bass of what's happening
around me,
syringing my ears of their
impacted orange wax: high
      in the renewed trees, the soft beak
of an embryonic sparrow

is chipping its eggshell
                blindly from inside
          with the heavy clunks of an axe-blade
felling the past. That resonant crash,
as of a tower-block
                being demolished,
is a baby in the park
clapping for the first time. And when,
at my feet, a twitching white moth's
                  borne aloft
on a convoy of ants, I can hear
the distant onrush of a wind-rucked sail, the ship
of a dead king
            being launched
                 on the bellowing seas

At Llantwitt Beach

Too much here
              for the eye
to hold on
              to: you look
now at the russet cliffs
          stepped and striated
                      into blocky
planes, like
      dilapidated
              half-pyramids; now
              at the maze
of glittering
              rivulets
zigzagging down
                  towards the sea,
  with a kite-tugging boy
and labrador
          angling across them
at tangents, kicking up
                  giddy radials
of spray;
          at the sea itself now,
that giant loom
      perpetually unravelling
              the striped tapestry
it's just woven.

            Compare
the kestrel
      hunting the cliff-top
as we clambered
                  down: so intent
      on her tiny
quarry, braced in the
                  coastal wind,
      she's
            bolted to the sky,
locked in fierce
            grace,
                        by far
      the deeper
                  reader.

Three Songs in Search of a Singer

I

Mythic

when I became fly
   you were lithe mottled trout
looming shadowy
   where I moved to alight

when I became trout
   you were sinewy otter
breaking and entering
   the secretive water

when I became otter
   you were tongue-lolling hound
snuffling for my spoor
   as I scurried to ground

when I became hound
   you took tall human shape
and leashed my throat round
   so I'll never escape

II

Thing-Song

the child running with his yellow chalk
is marking the things he wants to include
the things he encounters and wants to name
the tree the wall the lamp-post the lorry

the child marking with his broken chalk
the things he includes and wants to remember
the wall the tree the dustbin the scooter
making the names with his runaway mouth

the child chalking the things he discovers
the dustbin the flower-pot the gate the lorry
marking in yellow the lines of his running
making them things he can name as he speeds

III

End-Rhyme

I drank the wife's jewellery.
   I smoked the children's clothes.
The car went in my arm.
   The house went up my nose.

A Type of Ambiguity

What she envisaged as a vase taking shape
on the gently-revolving wheel of their days,

an ornament formed by their four
hands' dutiful moulding, he viewed more

as an elaborate code time and diligence
were bound to unlock, an encrypted grammar

of erotic potential to decipher.
So when, in that hotel in Florence,

after several tumultuous, synchronised
comes, he was moved to murmur *My love*

we've cracked it — and they collapsed back,
listening to the clatter of pigeons

fanning out across the piazza, like a deck
of cards being shuffled. It was then he realised

his words veered in three directions:
were vase, code — or their future — still intact?

Samara

As your mouth savours the word, tasting
for roots and connotations, they wind down
around us like worn clockwork toys; or spent moths
losing the power of flight, tail-spinning out of control.

Midges in the afternoon dark play out
their doddery cat's-cradle; and shambling home,
turning over old leaves, I imagine
a musty office at the terminal
where all our lost days come to rest: indexed
in boxes with dropped keys, bereaved
gloves, watches whose hands have seized
into place; unreclaimed belongings...

A lagged carousel in another time-zone
where our baggage shunts unendingly round.

Noncellations

scooped-out moon
                         an open bracket
the twitchy stars
                    legible for once
beyond London's amber-ish
                         permaglow
trashed on the balcony
                     we start to trace out
nonce-constellations
                    no less imaginary
than that first Babylonian
                      gesturing upwards
convinced he'd discovered
                      animals and deities
dot-to-dotted
               across the chaos of sky
 there's *Lada Minor*
                 a misshapen two-seater
Cassowary
           flightless malevolent
bird *O'Ryan's Balti*
                a Galway curry-house
The Snow Plough
              The She-Yeti
Empson's Beard
           A Map of Sri Lanka

tear-dropping earthward
                    The Willendorf Venus
as daubed by a tot
                    and why not abstracts
Kandinsky?
                    Rothko?
                    The Staveless Score
of star-notes ad-libbed
                    these chance-consolations
have no ceiling
                    fictive patternings
lost track of by morning
                    but copyrighted now
by the backwards neon C
                    of the moon
                              our open secret

Ouroboric

Parting that deathly
browned volume — in lieu still
of your brown thighs? — it falls
on me
          out of nowhere: crisp
diamonded snakeskin I
     dislodged from an outcrop
of Cypriot shore, flaky
and frail to handle but just
ghostable back to where
you basked and sipped
wine, smoking:
                    Repulsive,
take it back, it stinks.

          Quietly demoted
to bookmark, then forgotten
remembrancer, it coils
in wait three years, patient, hungry

until this doldrum morning in SE4, window
clawed across with sideways rain,
sorting books I want shot of:

out of nowhere
                    it springs
for me, loop of grey skin suspended
between pages like a frayed
rope-bridge, a smoke-ring hanging
                    years —

                    loose thread
with your body snagged up in it — biting,
clenching, vehement
                    that summer long —

(and didn't we form an oral-
hoop, mouth to each
                    other's tail?)

As though a snake could writhe back
    into its sloughed skin.

Myth of the Old Master

'The artist lies for the improvement of truth'
Charles Tomlinson

I

Working to the deadline
   of his body's waning duration
he paints on, despite the stubble of ice
   his greatcoat has grown, *maculae*
of snow that may well be his eyesight
   failing. If nothing else, let him complete
this landscape. He sits by the river
   beside the last, stubborn angler
struggling to hold captive
   a moment already gone, a play of bleak light
over water: grey-brown turbid on-surge,
   scant poplars like besoms, cigar-coloured
reeds and drooped stems. Let him complete
   this last winter landscape;
it replicates some region in himself.

II

   Eminence grise of this depleted river
the crook'd heron, catching no roach,

heaves herself skywards barely
splashing. Across February's stark
    diagram, dots of colour punctuate:
plodding to his vantage-point
    he spies aconite at the wayside,
nibs of green on hawthorn-twigs.
    He squints, trying to focus Art's
eroded lens; he wills the poplars
    not to come into leaf. But squats on,
staring: he can't paint round what's there.

III

How is it, next day, the men with ladders
    arrive, the tree-surgeons
in council uniforms? Theirs is a kind of art, too,
    this shearing and clipping
of incipient leaves; a kind of editing,
    or purging. They bend to their labour
bemused yet unquestioning: orders
    direct from the mayor. (And isn't the mayor
the Master's patron? Is it true
    the landscape, on completion,
is promised to his collection?)

IV

A day's grace before the leaves inch back;
   spring keeps seeping through.
But one good morning is all he needs, now
   the mornings remaining are so few:
to grasp back the origin, that speckled moment
   the landscape seized him
and he set out towards it, committed
   the first mark — as everywhere snowflakes,
like so many blisters,
   fell healing back into earth.

A Palestinian Donkey

Inured to the miraculous by then,
and in no rush to reach his ending,
he chose the least efficient means
of finally descending
into the city he had fought to cleanse.

Picture him now, astride
the blunt, fly-taunted ned, waiting for a ride
like a boy on a wind-
harrowed English seaside,
kicking his heels, unable to begin.

Three Domestic Interiors

For my mother 1945-2009

I

Waking Early in Winter

You yawn, that silent roar against waking,
straining your arms upwards like a diver
prepared to plunge. But I've crept here to warn
you — whatever white morning this may have been —
against wrenching your curtains aside
and squinting out, through the stuck kaleidoscope
of frost; or scouring in its glittered screen
a porthole. *Warn* my own mother? I'd mouthed out
the words, sweetened and consoling as our tea...

but when you crossed to the window, none came:
only white drifts of breath, and that clawing
at the throat which precedes tears. How could you not
make that parting, admit the snow-fraught day,
take in our three rabbits' carcasses ripped
across the lawn, each beheaded, crimson,
the hutch-door gaping open like a jaw?

II

Blackout

Like patient abrasion of an artefact
brittled with age, to grasp what's come to light,
you chafe the jaded Swan Vesta across
its worn sandpaper-page — in that dank
yellow box the crumbly duds outweigh
the live. We hunch around you in mumbling
suspense, like Neanderthals at their first glimpse
of fire. At last, a cursive scribble detonates
with a sound like velcro unseaming.

We recoil a touch, as you stoop, and communicate
the momentary, palm-cupped flame to a candle:
a glow-worm sacrificed to a glow-animal.

That abrupt blackout — moments before,
as though the whole house fell unconscious —
had you rooting through cupboards, rifling drawers
like an intruder to unearth these instruments
of sight, locating the children through a sonar
of name-calls and blindman's-buff gropings.

Soon enough, the living-room's ushered back
as a woozy apparition coaxed from tea-lights,
hushed for a moment as a séance
or Hall of Rest. But someone's dug out

a November sparkler or two, crackling-bright
and acrid: they arc-weld the candle-halos together
and sear a blurred initial on your retina.

Bereaved of TV, we soon lope to bed, probing
with torch-beam the ghost-mobbed corridor
of the stairs. I colonise the freezing sheets
inch by inch, resisting awhile the lucid dreams
that muster in the frostscapes on our window,
afraid to miss the sleep-balm of your last Goodnight;
then burrowing deeper, mining for warm,
I replay my body's initial unclenching
in the vivid, tactile blackness of your womb.

III
Process

  All the time
we slept, next door
lime-scale formed

  inside the kettle,
like microscopic
sedimentary layers.

  The ice-box
locked itself in. Microbes
in the semi-skimmed

were on the turn;
from black eyes
of King Edwards

feelers groped
and probed. A growth-ring,
like an unwanted

memory, accrued
beneath the bark
of the yucca. We slept —

as all the while
the cells staged
their dark proliferation

inside you —
irreversible
as the bulbs you gave us

bursting out
one January on
their petals of unseasonable

orange, flaring
like matches somehow
fixed in time.

from Proses for Hal Incandenza

i.m David Foster Wallace 1962-2008

I

Just as your life begins to assume the format recommended in the award-winning weekend supplements — your life-partner and offspring appropriately medicated, lawn plaid-mown with the aid of a theodolite, favourite reality show pre-recorded and shown on a loop — the visitor you've braced yourself against since early childhood is somehow a pixellated shadow flickering at the bevelled glass of your door, about to ring the bell: the policeman from your suppressed dream, helmet cradled like unexploded ordnance, bearing revelations you would harm anyone not to hear?

IV

(Breakdown)

Memory: waterboatman in a frozen puddle, rowing deeper far from any pond. Sense: the faint line of down between navel and pubic hair. Response: if witch-hazel smell, then pain. Dream: as demons scale fire-escapes to riot and loot in heaven, angels are parachuting down to aid the damned. Sign: THIS WINDOW OPENS ONLY PART WAY. Text: he opened his veins with his father's gold-plated fountain-pen, he claimed to be crossing himself out. Recording: *the*

black-headed oriole, a restless bird with beautiful cries, feeds on berries,
nectar, caterpillars, even butterflies in flight, taking the bodies only and
letting the wings fall aimlessly to earth.

V

(After Rimbaud — the speaker has made a counter-journey to his, from
Harar to London via France)

'I am a transient, not-too-downtrodden inhabitant of a metropolis
assumed up-to-date because every criterion of taste has been
disregarded as much in the architectural design of its office-blocks and
new-builds as in the panopticon of its urban planning. 'Monuments
to superstition' are subsumed within the retail-facades. Morals and
discourses are reduced to binary codes. These millions of beings
with no need to acknowledge each other's existence conduct their
educations, careers and retirements with such uniformity and lack of
will that the duration of their lives is several times longer than what
accredited statisticians have found to be the case in 'the Developing
World'. Hence, from my fourth floor window, I make out a new
species of apparition jay-walking through the fetid exhaust-fumes
these never-dark summer nights — a new breed of Furies haunting
the benefit-hostels as squalid as in their homelands, but everything
for them is no better than this: Death, like a social worker, removing
an unwanted baby; Love an unaffordable marketing ploy; the pretty
one with a police record, snivelling for a fix by the bins.'

VI

Prolonged sobriety — it turns out — is the strangest high of them all. Waking straight and staring out at rooftops and satellite dishes, first symptoms of autumn on the uppermost plane-leaves, stoned wasps pottering between them as if lost: it's all here, if you want it, things are exactly as they seem. The barest facts hold true. The bald mechanic mooching past keeps throwing his keys up and catching them again like some tiny clinking instrument; there's a ceremony inherent in the mundanest gesture today, the rhythm upholds us if we let it.

There's a pause between the simmer in the plane leaves and the second you feel the first scraps of rain begin to wetten your arms and hands, a barely perceptible hiatus: the moment opens if you listen for it, a mouth about to speak; it receives you in the downpour as you move through.

Last Living Speaker

I

(Royal Free Hospital, London, 2010)

After the stroke, English words
escaped you, like a coop
of cacophonous birds
you'd failed to tame.

The dialect of your distant
infancy — that landscape
of stifled voices — re-emerges

in their wake: revenant
of a long-
dead language,
it possesses and reclaims
your abandoned tongue.

II

(Von Humboldt's Expedition, Venezuela, 1800)

'In a cage
  scarcely permitting
his dog-eared, blue
  and yellow pinions
    to extend

we came upon Angel
  in the tribal village
hard by the Orinoco,
        kidnapped trophy
of their enemies'
    last demise.

From the beak
  of a macaw
I heard at last
      the cut-off tongue
of the Atures; met
  the mournful,
        gummy eye
of the oracle-bird
  through whose mouth
        so many voices
are now thrown.

Labyrinthitis

As Jonah is said to have lived inside the whale,
an ant lives inside me, lost in the coiled Underworld
of my interior, struggling for release. He tunnelled

down my ear-hole as I slumbered through
the nightshift; tiny explorer bent on expanding
the territories of Antdom, and claim *lebensraum*

for the coming swarms. My ear-drum suffered
no perforation, I dreamed some new slang utterance
was entering my vocabulary, relaying its urgent echo

towards my brain: he tinkers on the ossicles
in passing, clanging the anvil with bone-hammer;
he helter-skelters the slippery cochlea,

crash-lands in the labyrinth of the inner ear,
bearings dizzily lost. Three days and three nights now
he has haunted my polluted canals, his lamentations

a tinnitus in my skull: what else could this
restlessness be, this nonsensical whisper
that breaks my focus in whatever I attempt

and has me ranging these night streets myself
an ant, an ant inside a whale, seeking an exit, a
way through: to crawl inside your sleeping ear and speak.

The Ice River

'The Waterman, forlorn along the Shore,
Pensive reclines upon his useless Oar...'
        John Gay

That winter the bitter Thames froze over
our little Elizabeth could not endure
the cold. Ice seized the muscled river
so tight of grip, turned flow to deep-set stone;
the crammed city overran its banks; fair
and market jostled to the new-laid causeway,
vying for land too perishable to rent or own.

Mornings I'd loiter there — landlocked boatman,
my craft marooned ashore, cracking between
the frosty contractions. With river clenched
and stilled, my trade ran dry as a victualler's
in Eden. Pinched fishermen and portly
merchants alike would curse the chill, and pray
for swift reversal of this 'miracle'.

A chained bear, prodded from his winter sleep,
would stagger up in a parody of dance,
utterly morose and grudging; yet the traders
would goad him on, roaring, as they haggled
and bartered; children between the stalls
raising snowmen, conducting ephemeral wars.

There persisted everywhere such levity,
and carnival abandon, I could only
attribute it to this: their stark want
of time, pitched on slipshod ice, weighing
the imminence of certain loss with this
chance turn of grace — as all do, God knows.

But their prospering was my penury;
my wife and infants bore the unhappy toll.
Our little borrowing could not outlast
the snow: her swaddling proved her cerement.

~

On the ninth day, hoisted from its winter sleep,
a gross, red, apoplectic sun swelled up
over the spires and frost-sheened rooves of London.
None spoke: all moved in accordance with this sign,
and to hear — like eerie crow-song —
the faint creaks and fissures of the shifting ice.

Some dismantled the stalls and shelters
so lately improvised; some skidded back and forth
safeguarding wares. Chaos overtook them once again: fear.

Shuffling to my thawing skiff, thanking God
for His infinite mercy, I watched them
butcher the unruly bear for coats, gloves,
dog-meat. And in the ruinous sun,

the snowmen, suddenly old: how they shrivel,
and hunch over, weeping until they are gone.

Fool's Proof

As to our
        dead
(I have been thinking)
    they claim
                time
    back for us
in dreams
            never lucid enough
                or lasting.

So who could admit
                them
    to our sleeping heads
        but Him,
                overlooking
all, turning
        his vast blind eye
as they
        slip back
    to us — as new-forged
                    identities,
        plans of escape —
                    every
last moment
        they lost

Time and Motion Studies

I

To a Plane-tree, Queen's Park Gardens

Diminished in bearing, patchy,
inclined to stoop, you resemble nothing
so much as these drawn, shrunken women
who huddle beneath you, downing cans; from whom
everything is falling slowly away.

II

Subjected
   to the dense clamour
 these starlings send up
  in mobbing
the haggard oak —

  they re-leaf
its stark armature
    a half-season soon
you'd swear —

  he began
    to have a mind

for a more
    indelicate
rhetoric —

     III

Where they've demolished
half a terrace, a wall
bares etiolated
            paisley-flock
unaltered since
         '74; trace
of a family history
            briefly extant
before
the wrecking ball
         pendulums
back
    into play

     IV

The poem
has no place
in all of this?

All of this

has a place in
the poem

    V

Underground

     i)
ictus of white stick
  of the black geriatric
groping for open

     ii)
chance face
    at the departing window
whose stare
        you meet
and hold
    for as long as it takes
to go dark
     and disappear —
         bold
to find each other
     endlessly disparate
through momentum
      and filthy glass

iii)

Heaving tube at eight thirty, a man
    eighteen minutes late, no hope of seat,
watch-clocking; a flicker catches
    his edgeways eye and loops up, wavery: a moth
of all things, ochre-freckled, waking
    out of what raincoat-pocket? Pressed
and packed, nodding off or immured in papers
    no-one spots it but him - and soon as he
believes his eyes its done its flit. A moth
    was it, bypassing all our constrictions?

Alighting presently on Moorgate platform,
    he thinks he glimpses a signing-off:
smudge of dust and hemolymph
                ground underfoot,
    blurred X — but no time to bear this out
              with a backward look

    iv)

below hurtling feet
    how relentless, blind, slow
thistle bores through concrete

VI

Testimony

We used
three sieves
to filter the ashes,

to sift out
the bone-shards
and resistant
teeth;

to break down
the residue
to a flour-soft
dust

fine enough
to fertilise
their rose
garden.

VII

Bore the rushed brunt
of a bumper, that jay
did, spreadeagled yesterday

on the wet pavement,

his brutal arrest
granting this much by way
of bequest:

our unforeseen view
of tiny wing-feathers'
iridescent blue.

     VIII

I give it this:

that the poem's in
life, not about it,

a part of what we feel
to be here.

What's made of it,
however, I waive:

it stands
          for you

IX

Toddler in Garden

Barely abashed
   she stoops, hooping
her pants back
      then knee-
ward in a fluid
   jerk and upending
her head — unbrushable mane
cascading — to glimpse
the piss
      sluice down
   then back through
the grass, the tattered
   groundsel

X

Locu

   i)

Does gull's screeched diphthong
   creak like an unoiled see-saw
or vice versa?

ii)

Proof he's dyslexic:
   I find I hAT bAb felt-tipped
behind his bedroom door

iii) (*Long after Mallarme*)

'The chair is sad, alas —
   and I have consulted all
the brochures. Must fly!'

iv)

Leaves swept from wet pavings
   print after-blurs of themselves;
ghostly negatives

v) (*Outside the Lutheran Cathedral, Helsinki*)

Infantilising
   cartoon daubs on the bronze tsar:
bib and bonnet of snow

vi)

 Audibly undone,
   you replace the receiver
with a loaded click —

vii)

Crows and gulls on the
    football pitch vying for worms:
Manichean draughts

viii) (*For James Byrne*)

 Tweak from sill this wasp
    equipoised in death: wrought-gold
self-sarcophagus

       XI

Early November, and no hint
  of autumn
on the Lombardy
         poplar, though
  the park below's
     a shambles
of cut-ups, a
   vandalised
       ex's bedroom —

and on the street
  the pollards

like buckled

                   menorahs, candled
here and there
               with harsh
        crows

        XII

Crack-willows, silvering like water
as the wind veers
through; unbridled outgrowths
of lilac:
             they've all
but overtaken the tenantless
canal-boat, its flaky name
just visible:

GIPSY WANDERER

        XIII

Involuntary Memory

Alas, the old edition of *The Love Poems of Vidyapati*
    I was planning to buy and give to you
has the same musty smell as the porn magazines
I would find in the woods aged fifteen or sixteen
    and secretly abuse myself to.

XIV

Winter pollards

like stumps
of thalidomide
kids —

    Weeks later
I return:
         each club-arm's
sprouted hands
and articulate
            fingers!

XVI

In Avondale Park
the cottonwood trees
snow their seedy down
until the grass
lies white and woollen, sunlight
a-hover with fluff:

windfall of urban manna

Metaphormosis

In an archive of parched leaves, the cloud-bordered brindle unfolds her *mappamundi*, limned on vellum sunlight or touch would crumble —

Harcross Bridge: that seems, in this light, a wooden horse stooping down to drink, outstaring its reflection, as the mane of leaning men (spitting, flicking ash) baulk at theirs —

Never at rest, never swaying as such, the poplars perform their *t'ai-chi* —

Railings painted so hastily, the black municipal gloss entombs hawthorn-leaves, woodlice, a human hair —

The leather boxing-gloves abandoned on the footpath resolve back into horse droppings as you near —

In-and-out of umbrella brought wet indoors: that's how the take-off of carrion crows strikes you —

Her lace undies swishing in the sink, one lingual away from becoming *undines* —

Twin kittens play-tussle in a fluent, *yin* and *yang* ball —

Wind, hatching the butterfly painting from the nursery table — gaudy symmetry still runny — launching it: fluttering, faltering, fluttering —

Rough Guide

In Crouch End the people have no qualms.
There is no consensus on footwear
in Bethnal Green. What was the library
in Thornton Heath is now a greasy spoon.
Bayswater is famous for nihilists. Seven Sisters:
a mecca for the underdog. You cannot park
your van in Clapham North. A year in Raynes Park
does wonders for one's CV. Don't go
to Upper Norwood on Tuesdays. The feral youth
of Kentish Town shoot Ritalin. Redevelopments
are underway in Bow. Neasden has a thriving
New Wave scene. Jenga is massive on Primrose Hill.
Try Cricklewood for vintage uniforms,
Honor Oak for ethnic pulses. Urban badgers
abound in Dulwich West. For vernal picnics,
you could do worse than Willesden Green.
The dockers' slums of Bermondsey
now command six figures. Penge
is earmarked for a hi-tech face-lift. A blue plaque
for Italo Svevo is one of the must-sees
of Charlton. The charity shops of Purley
are a godsend. Racial harmony is alive and well
in Hounslow East. An Eritrean bookies has opened
its doors in Ealing. What was the cafe
in Thornton Heath is now a panini bar.
The loft conversions of Shoreditch are ironic

installations. Graffiti in seventeen languages
adorns the walls of Barons Court. Welcome
to vibrant Brixton: desirable, riot-free.

Lament of the Hackney Street Cleaner

'The most beautiful order is a random pile of swept trash'
        Heraclitus

Beenie tugged low, fluorescent
    tabard, steel-toe boots: just because
I traipse the streets all day
    collecting what you deem waste —
the spurned *disjecta membra*
    of your extravagant and otiose
lives — doesn't mean I have no soul,
    or lack cerebral exercise
as I trundle the cart, dustpan
    dog shit, or sweep the better-left
tesserae of leaves unendingly
    and pointlessly as Sisyphus
hefting his uphill slab. My compatriot
    Gorecki blares from the iPod
I salvaged from a drain
    on Kingsland Road, a densely
woven cobweb of sound
    I go enmeshed in; or sometimes
Stockhausen's otherworldly *Sturm*
    und Drang. They say a man's identity
may be pilfered now from his
    dustbin: is it so nearly
trash? Connoisseur of refuse,

gourmet of food-stuffs *'not finished*
but abandoned', it is me
  who plots the paper trail
of residue you bequeath, your 'footprint'
  on the criss-crossed palimpsest
of London. Your vacuity
  is summed up in this aftermath you leave
of Styrofoam, crisp bag
  and dog-end; your ethics
are a Readymeal flung
  in the gutter. Cardboard city
by the unsweet Thames, a teeming
  landfill of redundant
forms, moribund quotations,
  for all your techno-bluster and puffing
of your past, my circular evagations
  show me this: you're crumpling
around us, we've used you up, a container
  guzzled of content and dumped
aside. And so many humans too,
  subsumed within the rubbish, we're
  all of us mouldering, all of us
turning to waste.

Apocrypha of an Incomplete Angler

Reading the water they called it, the fisher
gurus I'd pore over at twelve; grizzled
soothsayers from Stoke-on-Trent or Bolton
whose back-page almanacs oozed a bullish
ur-poetry. Stalking a notional school
of chub or loping carp — evasive wraiths
wafting upwards now and then to graze
the surface with a *tell-tale* swirl, as though
brimming out from a mirror — you'd practice
a watchful reticence, making your reading
of the river and surrounding banks before
divining where to cast. Overslanting trees,
their torqued roots submerged; baize-green underlays
of weed; pockets of slack skirting a millpool:
these were the outward 'signatures' of fish-
haunts, but with no more surety of forms
beneath than the frogmen possessed, that August day
they dredged the gravel-pit for the missing girl
to no avail. That was years earlier, of course,
her white-wrinkled fingers too much to ponder
for an insular boy; I sat tight on my wicker creel,
mesmerised by water's unfathomable
fluxing, black as the inked-out page in *Tristram
Shandy*, wondering if reading and reality
would ever align: the tiny wand of my float
jolt under, and some radiant silver otherworldling

cross over into my hands. (Could a fish
even transform into the 'glimmering girl'?)

~

But nearer your age I wonder now — ascetic
seers of towpath and fen, pungent with *gentles*
and Old Holborn — what kind of men would keep your lonely
                                        hours;
spend each weekend nightfishing alone, neglecting
the wife and kids? Were all those accounts
of *mammoth hauls*, or monster pike you hooked but lost
apocryphal as mine? What secret compulsion
kept you bent there, unmoving, waiting
for your lines to make the sub-ghosts breathe our air?

The Lemon-in-Itself

Hovering
over the supermarket
fruit, nudging
for the yellowest,
    least marked
ovoid, hardly thinking —

turns *luminous* in the hand,
the one I grasp, a bulb
switched on, lighting
my senses all the way back
    to Sardinia
last spring —

backstreet of Alghero
trudging mapless;
    little lemon-tree
so violently alight with fruit
we stop to photograph
    it, like a celebrated
monument: you grab one

and bite it, sniggering back
the tart shock
of juice. That taste
    I get now, fondling

the porous fruit:

knobbled and gleaming,
    radiantly itself
beyond label, barcode, spin —

wasn't that the day
    we found wild boar
in the forest,

staring and stamping
    from behind
their electric fence?

The Duration

So many things have come apart
in my hands or somehow gone astray

they could form a museum,
a mausoleum of errings and shortfalls.

Like the one we drifted into when at a loss
that unrepeatable afternoon

we explored the historical market town
in the rain. The vitrines of stuffed curiosities —

faded hoopoe with its punkish mohawk,
a pangolin like an outsize fir-cone

endowed with limbs — amounted you said
to a *colonial mortuary*. The crude diorama

of a blacksmith's forge — ventriloquist's dummy
about to smite a horseshoe while his wife

and child look blankly on — was so unlifelike,
I wondered what a diorama of our lives

might resemble, a *tableau vivant* of Post-Everything
Ennui: mannequins of the three of us

watching adverts, waiting for the sky to clear,
my finger poised to hazard a futile suggestion —

like exploring an historical market-town —
locked into our stances for the duration.

Time Permitting

Summer has come to this: the sky invaded
by parachutes of cloud; abrupt random downpours
no sooner sheltered from than giving way

to precarious outbursts of sun. All season
has seemed this waiting for the season
to begin: waiting for the weather to include

us in its plans, or settle into patterns
no sooner framed than autumn will abridge
them, hauling down the coloured tents of summer,

moving on. It will come to this: swallows
giving way to the veering pipistrelle;
the ash-tree going to pieces on the lawn.

Cartoon Man

One minute sun, same ochre as the leaves
it's steeped through, gracing my stalled meander home
from work — the next: this strange attempt at rain,

hardly rain at all but just this gentlest
sprinkling imaginable, sparkling down out of a blue,
cloudless except for several oval clumps

like balls of screwn foolscap that've missed a bin
or ideas occurring to a cartoon man.
Am I him, then, skewed between two weathers,

clowning through this ticker-tape parade
of glimmers set up for someone worthier
to read a Sign in, some epiphanic

confirmation of faith — for him, perhaps,
the old asylum-seeker, fled from war
and displacement as I've fled driving-tests

and over-crowded tubes, but too busy today
spiking leaves one by one into his sack
even as others, other rusted hinges,

twirl unscrewed around him? Is there time,
in the end, or space in our memories

to pause and remember anything

so fugitive, uncatchable, each droplet
a tiny aperture onto a timelier moment,
a shapelier world which is nonetheless

this one I have only to live in?

An Old Philosopher in Brighton

The sea here's
          like life
at this age: an unstable medium
          better contemplated
than jumped into.

          Nor do the waves refrain
from teasing out their
quandary: they seesaw and can't
hold still, raking over the same
     shaky ground
          like a brooding
 divorcée.
                    Pebbles
time-sanded and honed
          to tiny abstract sculptures,
biomorphic Arps
                         suffer
the opposite failing —

like the pensioners sunken
in deckchairs they can't
                    easily arise from,
          these dense motes
overcome inertia and join
the scattershot fray

              only when hurled
to buckle a Coke can.

               Wave
and stone, motion and stasis:
                     a dialogue
that nullifies the rationale
               for action
and keeps me here — like the man
with the metal-detector
        hoovering the beach — intent
on combing
             for lost traces. (A jagged shard
from a gin
        bottle, for example,
abraded to this oval jewel.)

    Of the two piers — the one
aglitter and raucous
              with amusements,
a cut-price Byzantium
      of a future; the other
its gutted obverse,
              burnt-out
skeleton
        marooned offshore,
unrescuable as the past —
             which
in the end shall I take my bearings

by?
              The one, I suppose,
that at least yokes
land and sea, stone and
      wave: a suspension between
opposites, much like
              philosophy.

    The other's the silhouette
that history makes
    as it founders
              into the sea.

Book of the Giant

For Amaro

Giants at play, we are scouring beneath the hewn stones
that border this Cornish garden, heaving the rooves off
tiny communities where blood-spider and black ant,
networking ceaselessly, coexist in placid accord
with pottering woodlice; slugs that play dead unless nudged.

'And what do giants read?' I mock-harangue. *'Heavy grey
stone-books that open like this'* — dislodging the next slab
and wrenching — *'but all the words and letters keep scuttling
about: no wonder we giants never learn to read
but turn instead to roaring and devouring small boys!'*

I grab you and we roar together, loud as hell; then
listen for the after-quiet: a muffled crackle
circles the ring of pines, like an old record that can't
begin: peering up into the blue caldera
we stagger with invertigo: your pirouette of awe

says now we're shrinking: the trees are suddenly the giants.
'Pretend to be dead,' you whisper, *'like the naked snails
we found* — *then the giants can't bomb you with their pie-combs.'*
You grasp my thumb and parent me to an elder bush
frothy with blossom, snoring with hoverflies and bees.

We crawl under, where last year's threadbare leaves have bedded,
and you show me how it's done: stretch out straight, limbs rigid,
eyes goggling above. But what creeps over me, as we
lie there quietly, eavesdropping on insects and wrens,
is a faint premonition of what we're rehearsing,

a shiver of foreknowlege: one day they will chisel
a stone-page for each of us, unliftable rooves to hide
beneath — part then of the underground networks
we plundered; part of the humus that replenishes
giant-like trees. Mine will come first: will you at least be able

to unearth these days spent forming memories to live by?
'But Dad, you're moving: you don't even know how to die.'